What Is Electricity and Magnetism?

Exploring Science with Hands-on Activities

Richard and Louise Spilsbury

Enslow Elementary

an imprint of

Enslow Publishers, Inc.
40 Industrial Road
Box 398
Berkeley Heights, NJ 07922
USA

http://www.enslow.com

Enslow Elementary, an imprint of Enslow Publishers, Inc.

Enslow Elementary® is a registered trademark of Enslow Publishers, Inc.

This edition published in 2008 by Enslow Publishers, Inc.

Library of Congress Cataloging-in-Publication Data

Spilsbury, Richard, 1963-
  What is electricity and magnetism? : exploring science with hands-on activities / Richard and Louise Spilsbury.
     p. cm. — (In touch with basic science)
  Summary: "An introduction to electricity and magnetism for third and fourth graders; includes hands-on activities"—Provided by publisher.
  Includes bibliographical references and index.
  ISBN-13: 978-0-7660-3096-1
  ISBN-10: 0-7660-3096-2
  1. Electricity—Experiments—Juvenile literature. 2. Magnetism—Experiments—Juvenile literature. I. Spilsbury, Louise. II. Title.
  QC527.2.S665 2008
  537.078—dc22

2007024518

Printed in the United States of America

10 9 8 7 6 5 4 3 2 1

For The Brown Reference Group plc
Project Editor: Sarah Eason
Designer: Paul Myerscough
Picture Researcher: Maria Joannou
Managing Editor: Bridget Giles
Editorial Director: Lindsey Lowe
Production Director: Alastair Gourlay
Children's Publisher: Anne O'Daly

Photographic and Illustration Credits: Illustrations by Geoff Ward. Model Photography by Tudor Photography. Additional photographs from Dreamstime, p. 6; istockphoto, pp. 5, 8, 16, 26; Shutterstock, p. 22.

Cover Photo: Tudor Photography

contents

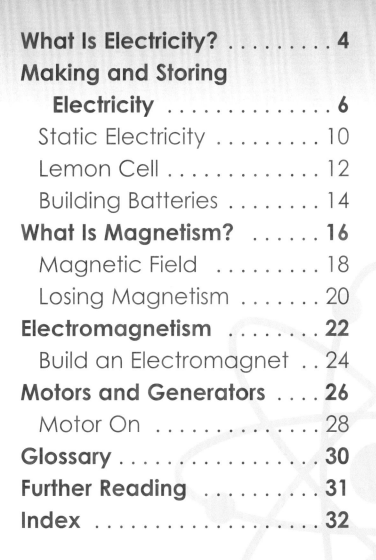

WHAT IS ELECTRICITY?

Electricity can produce energy to light our homes, cook our food, and run our computers and other electronic devices. But what is electricity?

Everything in the world is made of tiny particles we cannot see. We call these particles atoms. Inside atoms are even smaller particles, called electrons, protons, and neutrons.

Protons and neutrons make up the center part of an atom, called the nucleus. Electrons move around inside an atom. Sometimes electrons move from one atom to another. This movement, or flow, of electrons is called electricity.

Parts of an atom

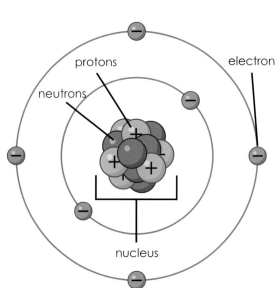

Positive and Negative Charges

Electrons have a negative charge and protons have a positive charge (neutrons have no charge). Opposite charges (a positive and a negative) attract, or pull toward, each other.

Things with the same charge (two positives or two negatives) push away from each other. If an atom has more electrons than protons, the electrons push away from each other. That makes electricity flow.

Static Electricity

When two different materials are rubbed together, electrons move. The more the materials are rubbed, the more electrons move. This creates a build-up of static electricity. Static electricity is at work when you brush your hair over and over so it stands on end.

The equipment inside an airplane cockpit is powered by electricity.

CLOSE-UP

ATTRACT AND REPEL

1. *If you rub a balloon on a sweater, the balloon picks up negative electrons from the sweater. If you then hold the balloon to a wall, the negative charges are attracted to the positive charges in the wall. That makes the balloon stick to the wall.*

2. *If you rub two balloons on a sweater, both balloons become negatively charged. They push away from each other when you put them together. Try it!*

positive charges

wall

1.

negative charges

2.

negative charges

MAKING AND STORING ELECTRICITY

Most of the electricity we use is made in giant power stations, but some is created by batteries.

Electricity is only useful if it can flow, or travel, where it is needed. Electrons can be made to flow along paths called circuits.

Batteries

Portable electronic devices, such as MP3 players, must be powered by electricity stored in batteries. Batteries store chemicals that react to release electrons. That creates electricity.

Cells

Most batteries have one or more cells. Every cell contains chemicals that create electricity. The amount of electricity a battery can create depends upon how many cells the battery has.

Small batteries with just one cell are used in machines that need only a small amount of electricity to keep working, such as a digital watch. Large batteries have many cells stacked together, called piles. These batteries are found in larger machines that use a lot of electricity.

◀ *The energy stored in batteries only flows when the battery electrodes, or terminals, are properly connected to a machine. But they are not safe to use if they are old or leaking.*

CLOSE-UP

HOW A BATTERY WORKS

All batteries have three parts: an electrolyte, a negative electrode, and a positive electrode. The electrolyte includes chemicals that can make electricity. The negative electrode is a metal case that surrounds the electrolyte. The negative electrode reacts with the electrolyte to make electrons flow.

Electrons flow as electricity from the negative electrode to whatever machine the battery is connected to. When the electricity flows back out of the machine to the battery, it returns to the positive electrode.

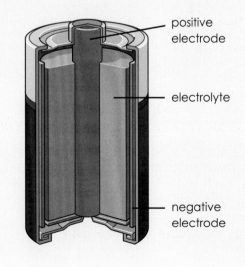

positive electrode

electrolyte

negative electrode

Measuring Electricity

Electricity flows from a power source in the same way that water flows from a faucet. We can time how much electricity flows from a power source each second. We call this measurement current. We can also measure the force with which electricity is pushed from its power source. We call this voltage (V).

Circuits

Electricity will only flow if it can find a circular path through which to move. This path is called a circuit. At the start of a circuit, electrons leave the negative end of the power source. The electrons then flow through wires and return to the positive end of the power source at the end of the circuit.

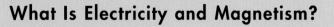
CLOSE-UP

SWITCHING CIRCUITS ON AND OFF

A switch works by making or breaking a circuit. If you turn a switch on, the electric circuit is completed and electricity can flow to a machine or to a device such as a lightbulb. If you turn a switch off, a gap is created in the circuit. That stops electricity from flowing to the machine.

- **Switch on (circuit complete).**
- **Switch off (circuit broken).**

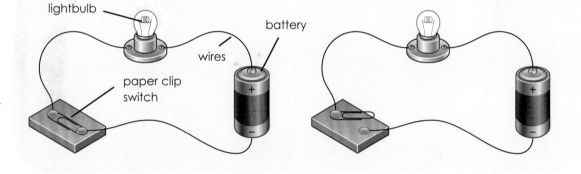

lightbulb

battery

wires

paper clip
switch

Electricity flows in a giant circuit from power stations to our homes and schools. The circuit is made of thick cables called transmission lines. The cables stretch across land, held up by giant towers called pylons. Electricity cables can also be buried under the ground.

Electrons move easily through metal, so electric circuits are usually made of metal wires. Electrons do not move easily through other material, such as plastic. That is why electric cables and plugs are covered with plastic. If we touched electricity we would get an electric shock. The plastic is a barrier between our fingers and the electricity.

Static Electricity

Can electricity flow through your body? Try these steps to find out.

You will need

- glass jar • thick card • pencil • thick piece of metal wire 5–6 inches (13–15 cm) long • thin aluminum foil • tape • plastic comb • scissors

1 Place the jar upside down on the card. Draw a circle around the top of the jar with the pencil. Cut out the card circle.

2 Bend the wire into a loop and carefully push the ends about 1 inch (2.5 cm) through the middle of the card circle.

3 Make a foil ball. Turn over the card circle so that the side with the wire ends faces upward. Push the wire ends into the foil ball. Cut a strip of foil about 4 inches (10 cm) long and half an inch (1 cm) wide. Hang it over the wire loop. Tape the card circle over the top of the jar. The foil strip tips should not touch each other or the glass.

WHAT HAPPENED?

When you rubbed the comb, it lost some electrons and became positively charged. When you moved the comb near the foil ball, electrons from the foil strip and the wire moved toward the ball. The tips of the foil strip became positively charged and moved away from each other.

When you touched the foil ball, electrons flowed through your body to the ground. These electrons canceled out the positive charge of the foil strip, and its tips moved back down again.

4 Rub the comb 10 times on a sweater or on your hair. Then move it slowly toward the foil ball. The ends of the foil strip should rise higher as the comb moves closer.

5 Hold the comb near the foil ball and touch the ball with your other hand for a moment. The foil strip tips should fall back down.

Lemon Cell

Did you know that you can make a battery from a lemon? Find out how with this simple experiment.

SAFETY TIP

You will need an adult to cut the wire.

You will need

- fresh lemon • stiff copper wire • paper clips • wire clippers • goggles

1 Roll the lemon along a tabletop. Gently push down on the lemon as you roll it. That will release the juice inside the lemon.

2 Put on the goggles. Ask an adult to cut a 3-inch (8-cm) piece of copper wire. Bend the wire in the shape of a U and gently push the sharp ends about 1 inch (2.5 cm) into the lemon. You are creating a circuit through which electricity can flow.

3 Unbend the paper clip to make it straight, then bend it into a tight U shape just like the copper wire. Gently push the sharp ends of the paper clip about 1 inch (2.5 cm) into the lemon. It should be next to the copper wire, but should not touch it.

4 Gently press the U-shaped ends of the wire and paper clip to your wet finger. You should feel a slight tingling sensation. That is caused by a small amount of electricity flowing from the lemon to your finger. Congratulations! You made a lemon electricity cell.

WHAT HAPPENED?

You made a single-cell battery! The acid in the lemon juice formed an electrolyte. The copper wire acted as a positive electrode. The steel paper clip acted as a negative electrode. By touching the electrodes with your wet finger you created an electrical circuit. Electrons from the electrolyte flowed from the steel to your finger and then down to the copper wire.

Try this!

Repeat the experiment, but use the same metal for both electrodes. You should not feel a tingle on your finger. That is because both pieces of metal are either negatively or positively charged. There is no pull on the electrons from one piece of metal to the other, so electricity does not flow between them.

Building Batteries

Can a battery be made from coins? Follow the steps to find out.

You will need

- paper towel • scissors • lemon juice
- 2 plastic plates • 10 pennies
- 10 dimes • 2 electric wires with alligator clips • voltmeter

1 Cut 10 1-inch (2.5-cm) squares from the paper towel. Put some lemon juice on a plate and place the paper squares in the juice.

2 Attach an alligator clip to a penny and place it on the second plastic plate. Place one of the paper squares soaked in lemon juice on top of the penny. Place a dime on top of the paper.

3 Repeat the "sandwich" of penny, paper, dime until you have used five pennies and five dimes. Connect the second alligator clip to the last dime on the top of the stack.

WHAT HAPPENED?

Each penny, soaked paper, and dime "sandwich" formed a cell. You formed a pile of cells, and when you plugged the wires from the alligator clips into the voltmeter, you made an electric circuit. The chemical reactions between the dimes (the negative electrode) and the lemon juice (the electrolyte) created a flow of electrons. Each cell produced a certain amount of voltage. The voltage made by your pile should have doubled when you doubled the number of dimes and pennies.

4 Each alligator clip has a wire attached to it. Plug each wire into the voltmeter. If you do not get a reading at first, unplug the wires and swap the voltmeter sockets they are plugged into. Record the reading.

5 Now increase the pile until it has 10 dimes and 10 pennies. What happens to the voltmeter reading?

Try this!

Electrons flow more easily when you use clean coins rather than dirty coins. Try the experiment again using very clean coins. (You can clean coins by dipping them in cola.) Your voltage should increase.

WHAT IS MAGNETISM?

Magnetism is a force that can push together or pull apart certain materials. Magnets are objects that can attract certain metals, such as iron or steel (which is made from iron).

The electrons in a magnetic material travel in the same direction. As a result, the tiny forces from each electron join to create a much stronger force—magnetism. The electrons in nonmagnetic materials, such as wood, travel in different directions. This cancels out their magnetic force.

Magnetic Fields

Every magnet has an area around it in which its magnetic force is effective. We call this area a magnetic field.

Making and Changing Magnets

Normally, the electrons in a nail spin in all directions. But when a magnet touches it, the nail's electrons spin in exactly the same direction as the

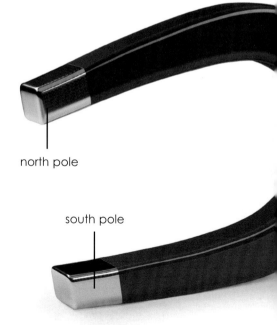

north pole

south pole

CLOSE-UP

ATTRACT AND REPEL

Two north poles push away from each other when placed together, as do two south poles. Their magnetic fields curve away from each other.

One north pole and one south pole pull toward each other, and even stick together. The opposite poles attract each other, and their magnetic fields join.

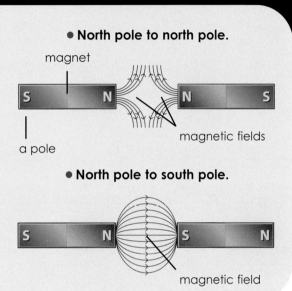

● **North pole to north pole.**

magnet

a pole

magnetic fields

● **North pole to south pole.**

magnetic field

A magnet's magnetic field is strongest at each end of the magnet. The ends of a magnet are called its north and south poles.

magnet's electrons. That makes the nail magnetic. The nail loses its magnetism once it is moved away from the magnet.

However, a nail can remain magnetic if it is rubbed along a magnet in just one direction. Objects can also be demagnetized. For instance, if a magnet is heated, its electrons spin in different directions and it loses its magnetic field.

Magnetic Field

Did you know that you can create a magnetic field? Discover how by following these simple steps.

You will need
- bar magnet, or several disk magnets attracted together • fine steel wool
- scissors • teaspoon • small, clear plastic soda bottle with lid • baby oil
- paper plate

1 Have an adult hold the steel wool over the paper plate and carefully cut off several pieces about ⅛ inch (3 mm) long.

2 Pour the oil into the bottle until it is almost full. Add a teaspoon of iron wool pieces and put on the lid.

3 Shake the bottle so the steel pieces spread through the liquid. Stand the bottle on a table.

4 Move the magnet to about ¼ inch (6 mm) from the side of the bottle. What happens to the steel pieces in the oil?

WHAT HAPPENED?

Magnetic fields form around magnets. Any magnetic material within the magnetic field will try to line up with the magnet. The steel wool pieces formed lines in the oil before they sank. The lines formed where the magnetic force was greatest. The lines were closer together near the poles, which was also where the force was greatest.

Try this!

Hold two magnets together to find their similar poles (similar poles repel each other). Then hold them on either side of the bottle, with similar poles heading toward it. What happens when the two poles are about the same distance from the bottle? What happens when they are different distances?

Losing Magnetism

How can an object be demagnetized?
Follow the steps to find out.

SAFETY TIP

Ask an adult to help you with this experiment.

1 Cut a piece of string. Tie one end of the string to the magnet. Tie the other end of the string to a tripod.

2 Cut two shorter pieces of string. Use them to tie the paper clip between two legs of the second tripod. The clip should be the same height as the magnet on the first tripod.

You will need

- 2 tripods or stands • strong, round magnet • string • scissors • paper clip • 6V battery • insulated wires with alligator clips

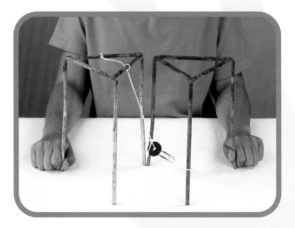

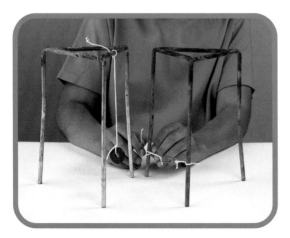

3 Move the tripods together until the magnet attracts the paper clip and attaches to it.

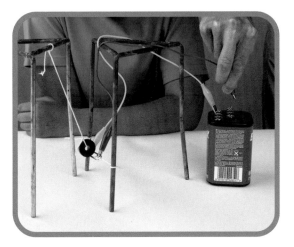

WHAT HAPPENED?

The paper clip became magnetic when it touched the magnet. You connected the battery to complete a circuit through the paper clip. The current made the metal paper clip warm up. The electrons in the paper clip then heated up and began to travel in different directions. They no longer formed a magnetic field around the paper clip, so the clip was no longer attracted to the magnet.

4 Have an adult attach onc connection wire to each end of the paper clip, then attach the other ends of the wires to the two battery terminals.

SAFETY TIPS

Do not touch the battery terminals. Also, do not touch the paper clip once the battery is connected. You will get a shock.

5 Stand back and wait. You should soon see the magnet fall away from the paper clip.

ELECTROMAGNETISM

When electrons move through wire as electricity, they create a magnetic field. This is called electromagnetism.

Electromagnets are magnets that are only magnetic when an electric current flows through them. Their magnetism can be controlled. When electricity moves past the atoms in a metal such as copper, the electrons in the atoms spin in the same direction. That creates a magnetic field.

When an electric current passes through a straight piece of copper wire, the wire's magnetic field is weak. The magnetic field can be made stronger by coiling the wire around a core of iron.

CLOSE-UP

COILS

Electromagnets are usually made of wire coiled around a core of soft iron. When an electrical current is run through the wire, the wire's magnetic field is trapped within the iron. The iron then becomes a temporary magnet.

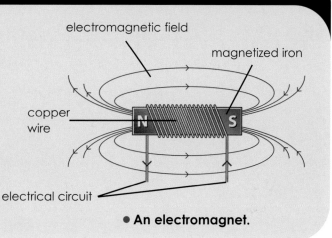

electromagnetic field

magnetized iron

copper wire

electrical circuit

● **An electromagnet.**

Off and On

Electromagnets can be turned on and off with a switch. The switch completes or breaks an electrical circuit. An electromagnet's strength can also be increased or decreased. Stronger magnetic fields can be made by running stronger electrical currents through the magnet, or by adding more coils of wire around the magnet's core.

◄ *Giant steel electromagnets are used in junk yards. Cranes can pick up large pieces of metal (such as old cars) by switching the magnet on. To release the load, they switch the magnet off again.*

Build an Electromagnet

How can the direction of an electrical current be changed? Follow these simple steps to find out.

1 Check that the nail is not magnetic by holding it to a pile of paper clips. You should not be able to pick up any paper clips with the nail.

2 Coil the copper wire 20 times around the nail. Leave about 2 inches (5 cm) of uncoiled wire at either end of the nail.

You will need
- large iron nail • 1-foot (30-cm) piece of copper wire • a 6V battery
- 2 insulated wires with alligator clips
- 10–30 paper clips • bar magnet with known north and south poles

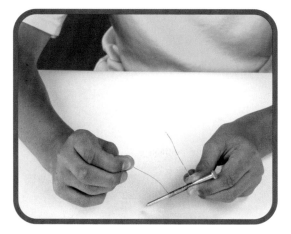

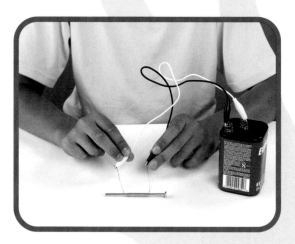

3 Attach an alligator clip from each end of the insulated wires to each end of the copper wire. Connect the two free alligator clips to the battery terminals.

4 Hold the nail over the pile of paper clips. The clips should now be attracted to the nail. What happens to the clips when you disconnect one alligator clip?

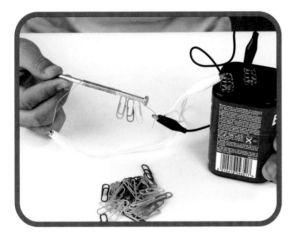

5 Reconnect the alligator clip and figure out which is the north pole and which is the south pole on your nail. You can do this by moving a bar magnet with known poles toward the nail. Now switch the alligator clips so each one touches the other end of the wire than it was touching before. What happens to the poles?

SAFETY TIPS

Remember, do not touch the battery terminals or the connected copper wire.

WHAT HAPPENED?

When you connected the battery to the wire you made a complete electric circuit. The electric current ran through the wire. That created a magnetic field in the iron nail, which attracted the paper clips.

The magnetic field disappeared when you disconnected the alligator clip, and the paper clips fell from the nail. When you switched the alligator clips on the wire ends, the current flowed in the opposite direction. This made the poles of the nail change ends.

MOTORS AND GENERATORS

Motors and generators are machines that change one form of energy to another. However, the machines work in opposite ways. Motors use electricity to produce movement. Generators use movement to produce electricity.

▼ *A lawnmower is powered by an electric motor.*

Inside a Motor

An electric motor usually has a fixed magnet around which an electromagnet moves. When an electric current moves through the electromagnet, a north and south pole are created. The electromagnet turns so its poles are next to the opposite poles of the fixed magnet (south pole to north pole, north pole to south pole). The electric current then changes direction, which makes the poles of the electromagnet switch. The electromagnet turns around again, attracted to the opposite poles.

CLOSE-UP

TURBINES

Nearly all generators are rotated by a turbine. A turbine is a little like a circular windmill blade. Turbines turn when a force, such as steam, pushes against them. Steam is made by burning fuels, such as coal or gas, to heat water. Wind and water can also be used to turn turbines. As the turbine turns, electricity is created.

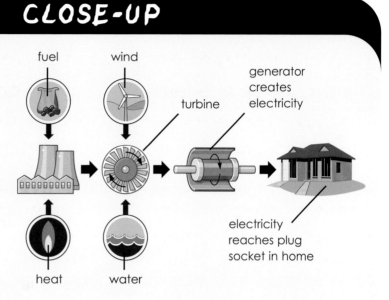

fuel

wind

turbine

generator creates electricity

heat

water

electricity reaches plug socket in home

● **Giant generators are found in power stations that produce electricity for homes.**

If this process happens quickly enough, the electromagnet will keep turning in one direction. We use this rotation to operate machines, such as CD players and electric drills.

Making Electricity

A generator uses a power source to turn a magnetic shaft inside a cylinder of wire coils. The shaft is a magnet. When the shaft turns, electrons inside the coils move. That creates a greater power source in the wire—electricity.

27

Motor On

What happens when you change the direction of an electrical current? Try this experiment to find out.

1 Position the two batteries in a row so that the small knob terminal of one battery touches the flat end of the other battery. Tape the batteries to the wooden board.

2 Position the two magnets about half an inch (1 cm) apart. The north pole of one magnet should face the south pole of the other magnet. Tape the magnets to the board.

You will need
- large wooden board ● masking or electrical tape ● 2 1.5V batteries
- 2 bar magnets ● 2-inch (5-cm) piece of thin wire ● 2 insulated wires with alligator clips

3 Attach an alligator clip from each of the two insulated wires to each end of the thin wire. Place the thin wire in the middle of the gap between the magnets.

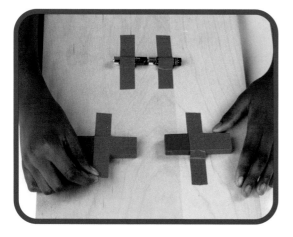

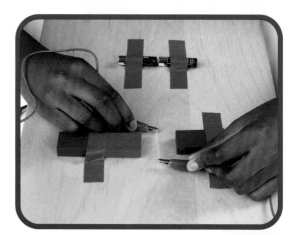

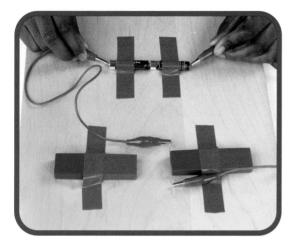

WHAT HAPPENED?

The wire was not magnetic until you connected it to the batteries. It simply lay in the magnetic field between the magnets. Connecting the battery turned the wire into an electromagnet. The wire's north pole was attracted to a bar magnet's south pole. The wire moved toward that magnet.

The direction of the electric current changed when you switched the leads. That made the poles in the wire switch around, and the wire moved toward the other magnet.

4 Touch the other two alligator clips to either end of your battery row. What happens to the thin wire?

5 Now switch the alligator clips so that each one touches the opposite battery terminal from before. What happens to the thin wire?

GLOSSARY

atoms—Small particles that make up matter. Atoms contain even smaller particles called protons, neutrons, and electrons.

attract—Pull toward.

cell—Part of a battery that creates an electric current as the result of a chemical reaction.

circuit—Circular path in which electrical currents flow.

current—Flow of electricity.

demagnetize—To remove the magnetism from a material.

electrode—Electrical terminal that carries a current into or out of a cell.

electrolyte—Battery part that includes chemicals that can create electricity.

electromagnet—An object that is made magnetic when an electric current runs through it.

electron—Particle that moves around the nucleus (center) of an atom and has a negative electrical charge.

energy—Ability to do work; for example, the ability to move something or cause it to change.

magnetic field—Force that exists around a magnet.

magnetism—A force that can attract magnetic objects.

neutron—Particle in an atom's nucleus that has no electrical charge.

pile—Battery made up of a set or series of cells.

power station—Place where electricity is generated, or made.

proton—Particle in an atom's nucleus that has a positive electrical charge.

repel—Push away from.

voltage—Measure of the force pushing electricity through a wire.

voltmeter—Instrument for measuring voltage.

FURTHER READING

Books

Dispezio, Michael A. *Awesome Experiments in Electricity and Magnetism*. New York, NY: Sterling (2006).

Parker, Steve. *The Science of Electricity and Magnetism: Projects and Experiments with Electricity and Magnets*. Chicago: Heinemann (2005).

Searle, Bobbi. *Electricity and Magnetism*. Brookfield, CT: Millbrook Press (2002).

Internet Addresses

Electric Avenue
http://www.aecl.ca/kidszone/atomicenergy/electricity/index.asp

Energy Kid's Page
http://www.eia.doe.gov/kids/energyfacts/sources/electricity.html

INDEX